What does God require of us?

MICAH

by Stephen Um

thegoodbook
COMPANY

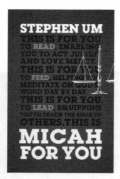

Micah For You

If you are reading *Micah For You* alongside this Good Book Guide, here is how the studies in this booklet link to the chapters of *Micah For You*:

Study One → Ch 1   Study Four → Ch 6-7
Study Two → Ch 2-3   Study Five → Ch 8
Study Three → Ch 4-5   Study Six → Ch 9-10

Find out more about *Micah For You* at:
www.thegoodbook.com/for-you

What does God require of us?
The Good Book Guide to Micah
© Stephen Um/The Good Book Company, 2018. Reprinted 2019.
Series Consultants: Tim Chester, Tim Thornborough,
                              Anne Woodcock, Carl Laferton

The Good Book Company
Tel: (US): 866 244 2165
Tel (UK): 0333 123 0880
Email (US): info@thegoodbook.com
Email (UK): info@thegoodbook.co.uk

Websites
North America: www.thegoodbook.com
UK: www.thegoodbook.co.uk
Australia: www.thegoodbook.com.au
New Zealand: www.thegoodbook.co.nz

ISBN: 9781909559738 | Printed in India

CONTENTS

Introduction: Good Book Guides

Every Bible-study group is different—yours may take place in a church building, in a home or in a cafe, on a train, over a leisurely mid-morning coffee or squashed into a 30-minute lunch break. Your group may include new Christians, mature Christians, non-Christians, moms and tots, students, businessmen or teens. That's why we've designed these *Good Book Guides* to be flexible for use in many different situations.

Our aim in each session is to uncover the meaning of a passage, and see how it fits into the "big picture" of the Bible. But that can never be the end. We also need to appropriately apply what we have discovered to our lives. Let's take a look at what is included:

⊕ **Talkabout:** Most groups need to "break the ice" at the beginning of a session, and here's the question that will do that. It's designed to get people talking around a subject that will be covered in the course of the Bible study.

⬇ **Investigate:** The Bible text for each session is broken up into manageable chunks, with questions that aim to help you understand what the passage is about. The **Leader's Guide** contains **guidance for questions**, and sometimes ☒ additional "follow-up" questions.

⊡ **Explore more (optional):** These questions will help you connect what you have learned to other parts of the Bible, so you can begin to fit it all together like a jig-saw; or occasionally look at a part of the passage that's not dealt with in detail in the main study.

➡ **Apply:** As you go through a Bible study, you'll keep coming across **apply** sections. These are questions to get the group discussing what the Bible teaching means in practice for you and your church. ⊡ **Getting personal** is an opportunity for you to think, plan and pray about the changes that you personally may need to make as a result of what you have learned.

⬆ **Pray:** We want to encourage prayer that is rooted in God's word—in line with his concerns, purposes and promises. So each session ends with an opportunity to review the truths and challenges highlighted by the Bible study, and turn them into prayers of request and thanksgiving.

The **Leader's Guide** and introduction provide historical background information, explanations of the Bible texts for each session, ideas for **optional extra** activities, and guidance on how best to help people uncover the truths of God's word.

Why study Micah?

We long for justice.

The world is not the way we would like it to be. Exploitation tells us that something about this world is off. Oppression tells us that things are not the way they are supposed to be. And when we are honest, our hearts tell us that we are not the way we are supposed to be, or would like to be. We easily choose greed over generosity. We easily choose our comforts over others' needs.

This longing for justice is not just a 21st-century reality. It's a human reality. Ancient people have always been, and modern people still are, exploring the ideas of fairness, mercy, and goodness. What should these look like? How do we experience them? How do we pursue them? What prevents us from experiencing these realities in every moment we are awake?

Micah—this Old Testament prophet sent to speak God's word to God's people—deals with these tough questions. And he tells us that God is a God who cares deeply about justice. He cares enough to judge injustice; to restore the world one day to complete justice; and to charge his people with doing good by pursuing justice:

> "He has told you, O man, what is good; and what does the
> LORD require of you but to do justice, and to love kindness,
> and to walk humbly with your God?" (6 v 8)

This is a book that resonates with our desires to see goodness all around us. But when we take the time to read the entire book of Micah carefully, we realize that God is not simply giving us a homework assignment about justice. The message for us is not simply a call to action to do good. God wants us to know the *reason* and the *need* for doing good—for his glory and for the flourishing of his creation—and to find the *power* to do it. As we read this prophet in light of the coming of Jesus, we find that Micah can inspire and transform us to do the justice we yearn for, and love the kindness we long to see.

These six studies will thrill and challenge you as you see how to walk through life in a way that honors and pleases the God of consistent justice and overwhelming kindness.

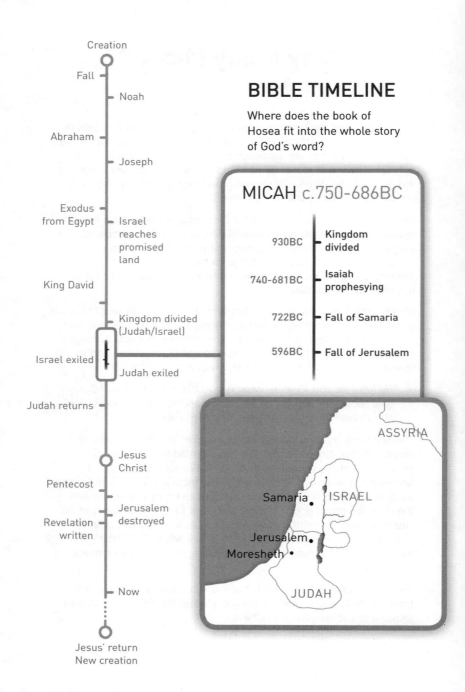

BIBLE TIMELINE

Where does the book of Hosea fit into the whole story of God's word?

Creation
Fall
Noah
Abraham
Joseph
Exodus from Egypt
Israel reaches promised land
King David
Kingdom divided (Judah/Israel)
Israel exiled
Judah exiled
Judah returns
Jesus Christ
Pentecost
Jerusalem destroyed
Revelation written
Now
Jesus' return New creation

MICAH c.750-686BC

930BC	**Kingdom divided**
740-681BC	**Isaiah prophesying**
722BC	**Fall of Samaria**
596BC	**Fall of Jerusalem**

ASSYRIA

Samaria • ISRAEL

Jerusalem •
Moresheth •

JUDAH

1 Micah 1 v 1-16
THE END OF IDOLATRY

⊕ talkabout

1. How would you define idolatry, and how serious would you say it is?

⊕ investigate

▶ Read Micah 1 v 1

2. What does this opening verse tell us about this book, and its author?

> **DICTIONARY**
>
> **Jotham, Ahaz, Hezekiah (v 1):** kings of Judah in the 8th century BC.
> **Samaria (v 1):** the capital of the northern kingdom of God's people, named Israel. Jerusalem was capital of the southern kingdom of Judah.

▶ Read Micah 1 v 2-7

3. What picture of God do verses 2-4 give us?

> **DICTIONARY**
>
> **High places (v 3):** places where pagan gods were worshiped.
> **Transgression (v 5):** sins.
> **Jacob (v 5):** God's people, the Israelites.

• Why is God coming in this way (v 5)?

Verse 7 tells us the central sin of the nations of Israel and Judah. There are "idols" in both lands—false gods being worshiped among God's people.

4. Look at what God will destroy in verse 7. What do these destructions suggest the Israelites have been making idols of?

The author Becky Manley Pippert writes, "Love destroys that which destroys the beloved."

5. How does this explain why it is loving of God to destroy his people's idols, even though that will be painful for them?

⟶ apply

6. What do the idols that Israel and Judah worshiped look like in your own culture?

    • Worship of wealth

    • Worship of sexual pleasure

God's people have not actively, definitively rejected the God of the Scriptures. They have deliberately, consciously added other objects of worship to their worship of him.

7. Why is this such an attractive option to God's people, now as then?

⊥ **investigate**

▶ **Read Micah 1 v 8-16**

8. What is going to happen to the people (v 16)?

DICTIONARY

Lament (v 8): expressing grief and overwhelming sadness.

Verses 11-15 list out names of towns that are hard to pronounce. Why are they included? First of all, because Micah is tracing out the path of the Assyrian army, which ultimately ends up taking over Israel. These are all the places that its king, Sennacherib, will come to in order to take control over these regions. This is the path of the means of God's judgment.

Second, Micah is also trying to show that even though these cities have hopes based on their particular location, those things will not come to fruition:

For example, "Beth-le-aphrah" means the "house of dust" (v 10). Micah says to them, *Guess what. You're going to ultimately roll yourselves into dust.*

"Shaphir" (v 11) means "beauty town," and yet Micah tells them that they are going to live in nakedness and shame.

9. What point is Micah making about their idolatry?

10. How does Micah show the correct response to understanding the idolatrous nature of God's people, and the judgment they deserve to face (v 8)?

⤷ apply

11. **Read James 4 v 4-10.** What should "adulterous people" (v 4) who love idols do (v 8-10)?

DICTIONARY
Adulterous (James 4 v 1): unfaithful to God.
Enmity (v 4): opposition.
Grace (v 6): undeserved kindness.

• What does the Lord do when his people do this (v 6, 10)?

12. How can we foster a church community that is honest about idolatry, serious about its effects, and quick to repent and enjoy grace?

⊡ **getting personal**

Is this how you treat your own idolatry?

"He gives more grace." How will this free you to repent right now… to mourn your sin right now… and to seek to change right now?

⊡ **explore more**

optional

▶ **Read Psalm 1**

What is the key to true flourishing—the antidote to and opposite of the idolatrous behavior in Micah's day?

⬆ **pray**

Thank God:

- that he speaks so honestly to us about what we are like.
- that when we humble ourselves before him in confession and repentance, he does forgive us and lift us back up.

Ask God:

- use your answers to Questions Six and Twelve to shape your prayers.

2 Micah 2 v 1 – 3 v 12
OPPRESSION, POWER, AND HOPE

The story so far

Micah warned the people that their injustice and immorality, caused by their idolatry, had left them facing the judgment of foreign invasion.

⊕ talkabout

1. Do you see yourself as an oppressor? If not, why not?

⊕ investigate

▶ Read Micah 2 v 1-11

2. What kind of behavior is Micah describing in verses 1-2 and 8-9?

DICTIONARY

Woe (v 1): sorrow and distress.
Apostate (v 4): someone who turns away from their religion.
Cast the line by lot (v 5): like flipping a coin to make a decision. In the Old Testament, this was a God-given way of receiving his guidance.

3. What is God going to do in response to this (v 3-4)?

4. For whom would this judgment of a reversal of fortunes be:
- bad news?

- a cause for rejoicing?

5. How do those described in verses 1-2 respond to Micah's challenge (v 6)?

- What would they rather hear (v 11)? Why, do you think?

▶ **Read Micah 2 v 12-13**

6. In what way does God follow rebuke with restoration?

➡ apply

Micah 2 is not saying that there is anything inherently wrong with economic gain. And it is not suggesting that you ought to feel guilty because of your gain and advantages. It is challenging us to come to grips with the fact that our possessions often come at the expense of someone who lacks the advantages that we do have—even the fair ones that can be celebrated. We can easily oppress someone else without an ounce of malice. It can be very subtle and yet very real.

7. What would the oppression in Micah's society look like in yours?

- How might you be guilty of it, either proactively or simply permissively?

- **Read 2 Corinthians 8 v 9.** How do we see in Christ the way to use our privileges rightly?

⊡ getting personal

Think about something you can use at your expense for someone else's good. Will you use it that way?

⊕ investigate

> **▶ Read Micah 3 v 1-12**

8. How does Micah say power is being used (or misused) by:

• Israel's political rulers (v 1-2, 9-11)?

• Israel's religious leaders (v 5, 11)?

⊡ explore more

optional

> **▶ Read Mark 14 v 53-65; 15 v 1-15**

How do we see both political and religious leaders abusing their power in the trial and sentencing of Jesus?

⊡ getting personal

Unless we are very self-aware, we don't realize the power that we have, nor the self-serving ways in which we can often use it. Here are two questions to ask yourself:

Do you treat someone with more influence differently than someone with less?

Do you use your age, or gender, or class, or education, or role to get what you want from a situation?

⬇ investigate

9. What is God going to do in response to this (v 4, 6-7)?

10. What does Micah do with the power that he has been given (v 8)?

- **Read Mark 10 v 42-45 and Philippians 2 v 6-11.** How is Micah pointing us towards the Lord Jesus?

➔ apply

11. What would you say to someone who says, "Power corrupts, so as Christians we should shun power and influence"?

12. "Have the same mindset as Christ Jesus" (Philippians 2 v 5, NIV). What positions do you have in the various areas of your life that mean you have some amount of power?

• What would it look like to use that power in a loving, Christ-like way?

🔼 **pray**

Praise Jesus by using Philippians 2 v 5-8 to help you worship him for his power and for the way he used it.

Ask Jesus to enable you to see clearly what power you have... how you currently use and misuse it... and ways in which you can use your power in a loving and Christ-like way.

3 Micah 4 v 1-13

THE LONG ROAD TO RESTORATION

The story so far

Micah warned the people that their injustice and immorality, caused by their idolatry, had left them facing the judgment of foreign invasion.

The Spirit-empowered prophet called out the political and religious leaders of the people for misusing their power to oppress the poor and serve themselves.

talkabout

1. How does our view of our future affect the way we live in the present?

- When you face a problem now, what difference would it make:
- if you knew it would be solved by tomorrow?
- if you knew that things were only going to get worse, for decades?

investigate

2. Out of 10, how hopeful and joy-filled has Micah 1 – 3 been?

▶ Read Micah 4 v 1-5

3. How does Micah's tone change in these verses?

4. What will "the mountain of the house of the LORD" be like (v 1-2)?

5. How does the restoration pictured in verses 3-4 reverse the portrayal of Israel's sin and God's judgment in chapters 1 – 3?

6. **Read Hebrews 12 v 22.** How does the writer to the Hebrews link Micah's vision to our faith as Christians?

⊟ apply

7. What would change in how you view your life today if you had a clearer view of your restored future?

- How will you remind each other of the heaven-on-earth Mount Zion that Hebrews 12 v 22 describes?

⊕ **investigate**

▶ **Read Micah 4 v 6-13**

8. What will happen to weakness and suffering (v 6-7)?

9. What will life be like before then for God's people (v 9-11)?

10. What will Israel need to remember, which the nations "do not know" (v 12-13, see also v 8)?

What will come to Zion, which means that God's time of restoration has arrived (v 8)?

▶ **Read Luke 1 v 32-33**

When did that time of restoration begin?

How does what Micah says about the restoration make the announcement of the incarnation to Mary even more exciting?

⇥ apply

11. What perspective on present suffering are these verses teaching God's people?

- **Read Romans 5 v 2-5 and James 1 v 12.** In what way do these passages reflect and extend what we read in Micah 4?

- What comfort do you tend to offer other Christians when they are in pain (whether due to circumstances or due to the consequences of sin)? Do these passages reshape your response in any way?

12. **Read Luke 23 v 33-46.** What had to happen on Mount Zion in order for us to be able to look towards the restored heaven-on-earth Mount Zion?

⬆ **pray**

Spend some time praising Jesus for what he did on Mount Zion.

Share any ways in which you are currently facing a trial, and pray for one another, that those trials would cause you to become more Christ-like, and more excited about the restoration that lies in your future.

Share any ways in which you are being called to comfort another Christian who is suffering, and pray that you would be able to do so in a way that points them to what God is doing now, and will do one day.

4 HE WILL SHEPHERD HIS FLOCK

The story so far

Micah warned the people that their injustice and immorality, caused by their idolatry, had left them facing the judgment of foreign invasion.

The Spirit-empowered prophet called out the political and religious leaders of the people for misusing their power to oppress the poor and serve themselves.

God promised through Micah that he would restore his people by bringing them to the place of dwelling and rule—but the road there would be painful.

⊕ talkabout

1. Why is independent self-sufficiency so attractive? Why do we aspire to be, and seek to appear as, self-made successes?

⊕ investigate

In chapter 4, we looked at God's vision of hope for his people. Restoration will come, but it is a restoration that will come through the pain of defeat and exile. Now, God reveals a picture of the kind of restorer who will achieve all that.

▶ **Read Micah 5 v 1-5a**

2. How does verse 1 describe the hopelessness of Israel's situation?

DICTIONARY

Muster (v 1): gather.

3. What do verses 2-3 reveal about the identity of Israel's rescuer?

4. How is this ruler described in verses 4-5a?

• In what sense is this the kind of leader that all people need?

5. Jesus described himself as "the good shepherd" (John 10 v 14). How does Micah 5 show us something of what he meant?

→ apply

6. In what different ways do people reveal their deep-down longing for a "good shepherd"?

7. In what ways does self-sufficiency get in the way of enjoying having Jesus as our shepherd?

☺ getting personal

What does your prayer life tell you about whether you see yourself as self-sufficient, or reliant on Jesus as your shepherd?

What would a reliant rhythm of prayer look like for you?

⊕ investigate

▸ Read Micah 5 v 5b-15

When the Assyrians invade (v 5), all Israel will ask for is rescue from their enemies. And God will deliver them (v 5-6)...

8. But what else does God promise to do with his people?

• v 7

• v 8-9

9. What will God "cut off" or "root out" (v 10-14)? How would each be something that the Israelites could look to for self-sufficient independence?

optional

⊡ **explore more**

How did each of these individuals need to give up any pretense to self-sufficiency in order to come to the good shepherd? And what did they gain from him when they did?

- *Mark 2 v 13-15*
- *Mark 5 v 21-43 (there are two individuals in view here)*
- *Mark 10 v 17-22*

⊟ **apply**

10. To what do we look to achieve independent self-sufficiency?

11. What would it look like for you to allow God to "cut off" those things, so that you can follow the good shepherd?

⊡ getting personal

If you go after any other savior, you're only going to be disappointed if you meet its demands, for it will not fulfill you. And if you fail to meet its standards, it will not forgive you. Jesus is the only Savior who, if you gain him, you will be satisfied, but if you fail him, he will forgive.

What difference is that going to make to you in how you respond to:
• your successes?
• other people's successes?
• your fears and failures?

⊡ pray

Choose different aspects of what it means for Jesus to be the promised good shepherd of God's people, and thank him for each of those aspects of his character and work.

Confess ways in which you need God to "root out" idols that you look to to achieve self-sufficiency; and pray for one another.

5 Micah 6 v 1-16
FINDING JUSTICE

The story so far

Micah warned the people—and particularly their leaders—that their idolatry, oppression, and injustice had left them facing the judgment of foreign invasion.

God promised through Micah that he would restore his people by bringing them to the place of dwelling and rule—but the road there would be painful.

God's restoration would begin to arrive in the coming of his Shepherd-King, whose background would be surprising and whose rule would be universal.

⊕ talkabout

1. What is justice?

⊕ investigate

> **Read Micah 6 v 1-5**

Here's how our scene starts: God summons his creation (v 1-2). He's gathering a tribunal before whom he can bring formal, legal charges—his "indictment"—against his people.

> **DICTIONARY**
>
> **Balak/Balaam (v 5):** Balak hired Balaam to curse the Israelites; but God caused him to announce blessings on them instead (see Numbers 22 – 24).

2. What does God tell his people to remember (v 4-5)?

• So what is the answer to his questions in verse 3?

❯ Read Micah 6 v 6-8

For an ancient Jew, the single most important thing in life was worship: to "come before the Lord" (v 6) at the temple with something appropriate in hand to offer and sacrifice to him.

3. What controversial possibility does Micah raise in verses 6-7?

• **Read Amos 5 v 21-24.** What is the answer to God's questions in Micah 6 v 6-7?

4. What has God said is "good" (Micah 6 v 8)?

• In your own words, what do you think each of these three requirements means?

▶ Read Matthew 23 v 23-25

To whom is Jesus speaking here?
How is he making the same point as Micah did?
How does this make Micah 6 more challenging for us as professing worshipers of God today?

5. How had God already exemplified to his people a passion to "do justice and to love kindness" (v 4-5)?

⊡ **apply**

6. How might we as the church today make the same mistake that the people had in Micah's day, do you think?

7. What would it look like for you to "do justice, and to love kindness":
• within your church?

• in your workplace?

• in your family?

• in your community?

⊡ getting personal

God's loving kindness and justice empower and motivate ours. If we walk humbly with our God, we will love to be like our God.

How are you actually going to love kindness and do justice? What practical changes are you being called to make?

⊕ investigate

The court of creation has been summoned and the defendants named (v 1-2); the standard has been set (v 8). Now follows the charge and verdict (v 9-12), and then the sentence (v 13-16).

❯ Read Micah 6 v 9-16

8. What is the content of the charges?

DICTIONARY

Rod (v 9): symbol of God's judgment.
Omri/Ahab (v 16): two kings of Israel who worshiped idols (see 1 Kings 16 v 21 – 22 v 40).

• v 10

• v 11

• v 12

• What are the modern-day equivalents of these sins?

9. What does verse 16 suggest is at the root of all this injustice and sin?

10. What is the sentence on this behavior (v 13-16)?

11. **Read Romans 8 v 1 and 2 Corinthians 5 v 21.** What position does Jesus take in this divine courtroom, and what are the implications for his people?

⮕ apply

Our lives are lived in a courtroom before the presence of a holy God. But the ultimate verdict is already in—Jesus has borne the sentence due to us for our idol-driven injustice and unkindness.

12. **Read Philippians 3 v 7-9.** What difference does knowing this make to us?

• What will this mean for us in the way we view our lives day by day?

⭡ pray

"He has told you, O man, what is good; and what does the LORD require of you but to do justice, and to love kindness, and to walk humbly with your God?" (Micah 6 v 8)

Thank God that he is himself the great example of a passionate commitment to justice and a deep pursuit of kindness—and then pray together about ways you sense you are being called to continue, or start, to do justice and love kindness.

6 Micah 7 v 1-20
WHO IS LIKE GOD?

The story so far

Micah warned the people—and particularly their leaders—that their idolatry, oppression, and injustice had left them facing the judgment of foreign invasion.

God promised that he would restore his people through the coming of his Shepherd-King, who would rescue, lead, and change the people.

God called his people to pursue justice and kindness as the way to walk with him, whose saving acts are the greatest example of doing justice and acting kindly.

⊕ talkabout

1. In what ways do people react to huge setbacks or great difficulties?

• Do you think there are better and worse ways to react?

⊕ investigate

> **Read Micah 7 v 1-6**

2. What is Micah reacting to (v 2-6)?

3. How would you describe his reaction (v 1)?

⤷ apply

What Micah is doing is to "lament." Lament is a passionate expression of grief and sorrow. To lament is to mourn, to grieve, to beat one's breast in anguish. In Scripture, "Woe is me" is one of the most powerful, deeply-felt phrases that can be invoked. It is only used in the most dire, grim, ruinous circumstances.

The Bible is not ashamed of lament. In the Psalms, 60 of the 150 are categorized as lament psalms—40%. The prophets lament as well. The book of Lamentations is devoted to lamenting.

4. Why is it encouraging to know that the Bible permits—even encourages—lamenting?

• In what way do you, or your church, need to hear this permission and encouragement?

5. What causes you to say (or think) "Woe is me"? How does that match up with the reasons for Micah's lament here?

• Is there anything that needs to change in your own priorities in life?

⊌ investigate

▶ **Read Micah 7 v 7**

6. Micah does not only lament. What three things does he also do?

⊡ explore more

optional

▶ **Read Luke 7 v 1-10**

How does the centurion look to Jesus, wait for Jesus, and trust Jesus?

Notice that this is what Jesus calls "great faith."

---

7. **Read Mark 15 v 33-39.** In what way did the Son of God's experience prove to be the *opposite* of what Micah had so confidently asserted in Micah 7 v 7?

It is this non-hearing of a lament that means we can be confident that Micah 7 v 7 is true for us. When we cry out to God for his help, we can look to the cross and know that God will not turn his back on us. That is what Jesus has already experienced, in our place. Jesus' prayer for his Father's nearness was rejected so that we can know that our prayers for nearness with him will never be rejected.

getting personal

You can lament in hope, for you cry to a Father who will never turn his face away. You can say, "I will look to the LORD; I will wait for the God of my salvation; *my God will hear me*." (7 v 7; emphasis mine).

Do you need to respond to a setback or difficulty in your life in this way right now?

Do you need to help support someone in your church to do this?

⊡ **investigate**

> **Read Micah 7 v 8-20**

8. What will happen, in the end, to:
• God's people?

> **DICTIONARY**
>
> **Indignation (v 9):** anger.
> **Vindication (v 9):** being proved right.
> **Pardoning iniquity (v 18):** forgiving sin.
> **Jacob/Abraham (v 20):** the "founding fathers" of the Israelite nation.

• God's enemies?

9. What will God's treatment of his people reveal about God himself (v 18)?

10. **Read Romans 3 v 21-26.** How does God both justly punish his people's sin, and compassionately forgive and restore his people?

11. The name Micah means "Who is like God?" which is the question he asks in verse 18. What is the answer, and why?

➔ apply

12. If we forget either the reality and seriousness of our sin, or the completeness of our forgiveness, how will this affect:

• our relationship with God?

• our relationship with others? (Hint: The way we relate to God tends to shape the way we interact with those around us.)

13. If you had to sum up in a sentence what the Holy Spirit has shown you through the prophet Micah as you have studied his book, what would it be?

⊡ getting personal

And what difference is that sentence you just wrote down making to your life?

⬆ pray

Share your answers to Question Thirteen and use them to prompt you to praise God, and to ask him to enable you to walk humbly with him.

What does God require of us?

Micah

LEADER'S GUIDE

Leader's Guide

INTRODUCTION

Leading a Bible study can be a bit like herding cats—everyone has a different idea of what the passage could be about, and a different line of enquiry that they want to pursue. But a good group leader is more than someone who just referees this kind of discussion. You will want to:

- correctly understand and handle the Bible passage. But also...

- encourage and train the people in your group to do this for themselves. Don't fall into the trap of spoon-feeding people by simply passing on the information in the Leader's Guide. Then...

- make sure that no Bible study is finished without everyone knowing how the passage is relevant for them. What changes do you all need to make in the light of the things you have been learning? And finally...

- encourage the group to turn all that has been learned and discussed into prayer.

Your Bible-study group is unique, and you are likely to know better than anyone the capabilities, backgrounds and circumstances of the people you are leading. That's why we've designed these guides with a number of optional features. If they're a quiet bunch, you might want to spend longer on *talkabout*. If your time is limited, you can choose to skip *explore more*, or get people to look at these questions at home. Can't get enough of Bible study? Well, some studies have optional extra homework projects. As leader, you can adapt and select the material to the needs of your particular group.

So what's in the Leader's Guide?

The main thing that this Leader's Guide will help you to do is to understand the major teaching points in the passage you are studying, and how to apply them. As well as guidance for the questions, the Leader's Guide for each session contains the following important sections:

THE BIG IDEA

One or two key sentences will give you the main point of the session. This is what you should be aiming to have fixed in people's minds as they leave the Bible study. And it's the point you need to head back toward when the discussion goes off at a tangent.

SUMMARY

An overview of the passage, including plenty of useful historical background information.

OPTIONAL EXTRA

Usually this is an introductory activity that ties in with the main theme of the Bible study, and is designed to "break the ice" at the beginning of a session. Or it may be a "homework project" that people can tackle during the week.

So let's take a look at the various different features of a Good Book Guide:

⊕ talkabout

Each session kicks off with a discussion question, based on the group's opinions or experiences. It's designed to get people talking and thinking in a general way about the main subject of the Bible study.

⬇ investigate

The first thing you and your group need to know is what the Bible passage is about, which is the purpose of these questions. But watch out—people may come up with answers based on their experiences or teaching they have heard in the past, without referring to the passage at all. It's amazing how often we can get through a Bible study without actually looking at the Bible! If you're stuck for an answer, the Leader's Guide contains guidance for questions. These are the answers to direct your group to. This information isn't meant to be read out to people—ideally, you want them to discover these answers from the Bible for themselves. Sometimes there are optional follow-up questions (see ⊻ in guidance for questions) to help you help your group get to the answer.

⬆ explore more

These questions generally point people to other relevant parts of the Bible. They are useful for helping your group to see how the passage fits into the "big picture" of the whole Bible. These sections are OPTIONAL—only use them if you have time. Remember that it's better to finish in good time having really grasped one big thing from the passage, than to try and cram everything in.

➔ apply

We want to encourage you to spend more time working at application—too often, it is simply tacked on at the end. In the Good Book Guides, apply sections are mixed in with the investigate sections of the study. We hope that people will realize that application is not just an optional extra, but rather, the whole purpose of studying the

Bible. We do Bible study so that our lives can be changed by what we hear from God's word. If you skip the application, the Bible study hasn't achieved its purpose.

These questions draw out practical lessons that we can all learn from the Bible passage. You can review what has been learned so far, and think about practical differences that this should make in our churches and our lives. The group gets the opportunity to talk about what they personally have learned.

⬚ getting personal

These can be done at home, but it is well worth allowing a few moments of quiet reflection during the study for each person to think and pray about specific changes they need to make in their own lives. Why not have a time for reporting back at the beginning of the following session, so that everyone can be encouraged and challenged by one another to make application a priority?

⬆ pray

In Acts 4 v 25-30 the first Christians quoted Psalm 2 as they prayed in response to the persecution of the apostles by the Jewish religious leaders. Today however, it's not as common for Christians to base prayers on the truths of God's word as it once was. As a result, our prayers tend to be weak, superficial and self-centered rather than bold, visionary and God-centered.

The prayer section is based on what has been learned from the Bible passage. How different our prayer times would be if we were genuinely responding to what God has said to us through his word.

1 Micah 1 v 1-16
THE END OF IDOLATRY

THE BIG IDEA
Idolatry—worshiping something other than, or as well as, the true, awesome, merciful God—delivers to us nothing except God's judgment. So as his people, we must identify and repent of our idols, knowing that he always stands ready to extend grace to us.

SUMMARY
The opening verse puts this prophecy in context. Micah is speaking "the word of the Lord" during the 8th century BC (v 1). We know this from the reference to three kings from Judah, the southern section of the promised land (v 1). God's people had divided two centuries previously, during the reign of Solomon's son Rehoboam. Ever since, there had been two kingdoms: Israel to the north, centered on the capital of Samaria; Judah to the south, with Jerusalem as its capital. Micah says that this message is "concerning Samaria and Jerusalem"—i.e. it's for both Israel and Judah.

In chapter 1 Micah first describes the judgment for idolatry (v 1-9). God is coming to "tread upon the high places of the earth" (v 3)—where foreign gods were worshiped—and to destroy the associated idols of wealth and sex which these false religions promoted (v 7). But as we'll see in this study, this is ultimately done in love: God will judge his people now, to remove their idols and return them to himself, so that they will not be left with their idols and be destroyed *by* them, and along *with* them, at his final judgment.

Second, Micah describes attachment to idolatry (v 10-15). An idol captures the

hearts and imaginations of those who worship it, and as such it influences and shapes the worshiper—both on an individual level and as a society. In these verses Micah turns this truth on its head. The description of God's judgment in verses 10-12 uses deliberate puns on place names to describe the ironic nature of their eventual destruction: the very thing that each place worships will be the source of its destruction (see note on pages 9-10).

Lastly, Micah points to a rescue from idolatry. In verses 8-9 Micah acts as an advocate between God and the people. But he can't change anything. He can only lament; but Jesus came to remove our lament and act as our effective ambassador. For Christians today, we are called to turn from our idolatry in the light of Christ's ambassadorial work in the way described in James 4 v 1-10.

If we are to grasp the rest of Micah's message to the Israelites and to us, we need in this first study to think carefully about their idolatry and ours. It's worth pushing your group to seriously consider their own idols, and to allow good time for reflection and application.

OPTIONAL EXTRA
To help establish the historical context of the book of Micah, write some major Bible events and characters on a series of post-it notes, and get your group to work together to put them in the right order, and guess approximate dates. Include the following, plus anything else your group has studied recently (some dates are approximate): Abraham (2000 BC), the Exodus (1500 BC),

the time of the Judges (1300 – 1100 BC), King David's reign (1000 BC), the Kingdom divides (930 BC), Elijah (860 BC), Micah (730 BC), the fall of Samaria to Assyria (722 BC), the fall of Jerusalem to Babylon (598 BC), Nehemiah rebuilds Jerusalem (440 BC), the birth of Jesus.

GUIDANCE FOR QUESTIONS

1. How would you define idolatry, and how serious would you say it is? Take the question in two parts. Don't seek the "correct answer" at this stage. Your group may define idolatry in an overly reductive way (e.g. "A statue that people in ancient times thought was a god") or a more biblical way—something we worship, serve, and trust in addition to or in place of the true, living God. Equally, they may view it as serious in the sense of what it does to the worshiper (enslaves them, since it never delivers the satisfaction, peace, etc that it offers) or in how God views it (worthy of judgment). You could return to discuss and amend your answers after Q4, 9 or 12.

2. What does this opening verse tell us about this book, and its author?
- It is "the word of the Lord." In many of the other prophets, the introductory phrase differs: "the word of Amos" (for example). Micah's point here is to call us right from the beginning to remember that these are God's words.
- God's words come through Micah, at a particular historical point in time.
- Micah's prophecy came during the reigns of three kings of Judah—Jotham, Ahaz, and Hezekiah. (No kings of Israel are mentioned. In other words, they are not even worthy to be mentioned in what is happening here because of the idolatrous activity they are involved in as a nation.)
- This word is for both Samaria and

Jerusalem—that is, both the northern kingdom of Israel (with Samaria as its capital) and the southern kingdom of Judah (with Jerusalem as its capital).

3. What picture of God do verses 2-4 give us?
- v 2: He is coming down as a witness against the inhabitants of the earth (primarily his people).
- v 3: He is coming to "tread upon the high places" (that is, places for idol-worship). This is the God who destroys.
- v 4: He is a God who melts mountains and splits valleys. Here is a glimpse of the God of incomparable power over his creation.

- **Why is God coming in this way (v 5)?** Because his people have sinned. God is coming in power to judge his people and destroy their false worship (notice that Jerusalem is described as a "high place" of Judah—that is, the inhabitants of the city are engaging in idol-worship).

4. Look at what God will destroy in verse 7. What do these destructions suggest the Israelites have been making idols of?
- "Her carved images shall be beaten to pieces"—they are choosing to break the second commandment (not to make images of God). If people choose to worship God in a way that is different than the one he sets out, very soon they will choose to worship a god who is different than the one who is real.
- "Her wages shall be burned with fire"— their idolatry centers upon wealth. They worship their wages.
- "To the fee of a prostitute they shall return"—many pagan religious temples of the time boasted shrine prostitutes. It looks as though God's people were worshiping sexual experience.

5. How does this [the idea that "Love destroys that which destroys the beloved"] explain why it is loving of God to destroy his people's idols, even though that will be painful for them? Because if they continue to worship idols and think that idols will give them what they need, they will never return to him to find forgiveness from and life with him. God will allow to destroy those things that are destroying them, detaching them from the ability to think wealth, sex, etc will deliver what they need. That way, they will not end up worshiping their idols rather than him, and so find themselves destroyed in his final judgment. Just as parents do not wish to see their children engaged in activities which will harm them—and may remove those activities from them, despite their children's protestations—so God acts here in judgment out of love, not out of hate.

6. APPLY: What do the idols that Israel and Judah worshiped look like in your own culture?
• **Worship of wealth**
• **Worship of sexual pleasure**
Make sure your group does not only identify the way wealth and sex are worshiped "by other people," but also by you as individuals. It is always far easier to speak of others' idolatry than our own!

7. APPLY: Why is this [worshiping idols in addition to rather than instead of God] such an attractive option to God's people, now as then? Because it enables us to think that we are being faithful to God, good followers of his, even though we are not. We can feel that we can have "the best of both worlds"—God's blessings without the cost of single-minded devotion to him, and what our idols promise in terms of comfort, satisfaction, security, etc. It

actually takes far more courage to reject the God of the Bible than it does to ask him to co-exist with idols. But this is still spiritual adultery.

8. What is going to happen to the people (v 16)? "They shall go from you into exile." This may come in the generation of these people's children, but this is what is coming. They will be taken from the land God has given them and blessed them in; they will be defeated and exiled. This is exactly what took place—the Assyrians (Micah prophesies their invasion in verses 11-15) conquered Israel in 722 BC and exiled many of the people; Judah was likewise invaded and its people exiled in 598 BC by the Babylonians.

9. What point is Micah making about their idolatry? Verses 10-15 use deliberate puns that describe the ironic nature of the eventual destruction: the very thing that each place worships will be the source of its destruction and the place where its judgment is most clearly seen. When an idol does not deliver anything except division and disappointment, frustration and misery, it is the place where the absurdity of worshiping anything other than the Creator is clearly shown.

10. How does Micah show the correct response to the idolatrous nature of God's people, and the judgment they deserve to face (v 8)? He laments, he wails, and he enacts/embodies the shame of the people by going "stripped and naked." He mourns because he understands that judgment is coming. In a sense, he is acting on behalf of the people—but (unlike Christ) he can do no more than mourn for them. The image is powerful though—as everyone else in the land continues with life, worshiping wealth and sex alongside God, Micah is doing what they all should be doing, for he knows what is coming.

11. APPLY: Read James 4 v 4-10. What should "adulterous people" (v 4) who love idols do (v 8-10)?

- Come near to God (v 8a). They should admit how they have been unfaithful, and come back to loving and serving God.
- Turn from sin (v 8b). They must change their behavior and thoughts ("hands … hearts"). Repentance involves a real change: a turning away from or forsaking of sin.
- Feel the weight of their idolatry (v 9). Genuine repentance means grieving, even weeping, about what has happened (as Micah did, Micah 1 v 8). James is not saying people can never be joyful (see 1 v 2). But there should be a place for seriousness and grief about sin.
- Humble themselves (v 10): The only right response to a proper realization of oneself as being an idolater is humility—accepting who we are, and what we therefore deserve from God, and that we therefore have nothing to bring to him in defense or to bargain with him. Humility is a prerequisite for repentance and for asking for forgiveness and restoration.

- **What does the Lord do when his people do this (v 6, 10)?**
  - v 6: He gives more grace. He is always willing to extend mercy to a repentant sinner. You cannot cause God to run out of a desire or ability to forgive you.
  - v 10: He will exalt you. God calls his people to humble themselves not to keep them down, but to lift them up.

12. APPLY: How can we foster a church community that is honest about idolatry, serious about its effects, and

quick to repent and enjoy grace? Discuss how you can be honest with each other; how you can make sure you do not belittle or excuse the sins of others when they tell you they are struggling; how and when you need to challenge each other to repent, and remind each other of grace.

EXPLORE MORE
Read Psalm 1. What is the key to true flourishing—the antidote to and opposite of the idolatrous behavior in Micah's day? An idol captures the hearts and imaginations of those who worship it. To flourish—to be "blessed"—we must allow the Lord God to capture our hearts and minds, through his word. This requires us both to consciously reject following those who worship idols (v 1), remembering where that life leads (v 4-5), and, positively, to delight in God's word: to meditate upon it, so that this is what shapes our minds, stirs our affections, and therefore directs our lives, resulting in happiness. Everyone is being influenced and shaped by something—either by God's word or by the empty promises of an idol. So the key to true flourishing is to read, and enjoy, and think about, and recall, the promises of God's word.

2 Micah 2 v 1 – 3 v 12
OPPRESSION, POWER, AND HOPE

THE BIG IDEA

It is easy for us to oppress others without realizing it, and to use our power to take advantage of others without us realizing it—but God sees, and cares. Our privilege and power should be used to serve others, not ourselves—just as Jesus used his infinite power to serve us.

SUMMARY

These two chapters contain more uncomfortable truths for modern readers. Chapter 2 focuses on economic oppression, with the opening verse declaring "woe" on the wicked. Yet the description that follows encompasses both those who scheme deliberate evil (2 v 1, 8), and those who use legal, yet ultimately unjust means to seize other people's homes and livelihoods for their own gain (v 2, 9—referring to repossessions as the consequence of defaulting on a loan).

This chapter should cause us to consider our own role in "the system." Inequality, in every sense of that word, is worse today than it has ever been. We can either choose to be real with it or just close our eyes and ignore the reality that constantly surrounds us. Sadly, those in Micah's day chose the latter (v 6, 11).

However, this chapter also declares good news for anyone who is poor and without hope. God is on their side. A great reversal of fortunes is coming (v 3-4). A Shepherd is on his way, who will gather his people together and give all of them "pasture"—all

they need, for all of them (v 12).

Chapter 3 focuses on the abuse of power, defined as taking the influence God has given you for the sake of the common good, and using it against others for selfish gain. Both Israel's political leaders (3 v 1-3, 9-11) and religious leaders (v 5, 11) are guilty of this. Yet whereas the false prophets will say what the people paying them want to hear (v 5), Micah uses the power of the Spirit to pursue justice bravely, and declare truth unsparingly (v 8). It's important to remember that power is a gift that can be used for human flourishing. Power is not intrinsically sinful; it's the abuse of power that needs to be addressed.

Ultimately, we'll see in this study that Christ is our Savior and model in the way he made himself poor in order to make us rich (2 Corinthians 8 v 9), and used his power to serve us (Mark 10 v 42-45 and Philippians 2 v 6-11).

OPTIONAL EXTRA

Linking with Q7: Show your group a short video to help them understand the reality of economic oppression in your society today. A search on YouTube along the lines of "What's it like to be poor in America?" (or whichever country you live in) should throw up plenty of suitable results. Alternatively, ask a group member to research the topic before your session, and to come with statistics and stories to share with the others.

GUIDANCE FOR QUESTIONS
1. Do you see yourself as an oppressor?

If not, why not? When we think about oppression, our minds typically drift towards some caricature of evil—somebody with malice in their eyes who intentionally preys on the weak. Sometimes oppression does take that form. But (as Micah will show us) oppression can be implicit and subtle. We can enjoy the benefits of structural oppression even as we decry overt oppression. The aim of this question is to have a slightly uncomfortable discussion, on which the rest of the study will then help to supply clarity on!

2. What kind of behavior is Micah describing in verses 1-2 and 8-9? Unjust oppression of others in society. Verse 1 describes a calculated, wicked oppression. These people "work evil on their beds." Some do evil even in their sleep because they are thinking about it so much. Verses 2 and 9 describe oppression that could be less deliberate and obvious. "They covet fields and seize them" (v 2)—in an agrarian society, a person's fields would have been the means of opportunity and how they made a living and a life for themselves and their family. So if someone's field was seized, even if it was not out of malice and explicit ill intent, they would be severely crippled and economically put at a disadvantage. "The women of my people you drive out from their delightful houses; from their young children you take away my splendor forever" (v 9): this is speaking of the way the vulnerable—women and children—were allowed to become disadvantaged by the systems and conduct of the wealthier and more powerful. Verse 8 paints a picture of people who see everything as potential "plunder" for themselves. They will take advantage of people who do not look at the world that way (have "no thought of war") to take what they can.

3. What is God going to do in response to this (v 3-4)? He is going to bring an end to this oppression. There will be "disaster" for those who are the oppressors (v 3). And he is going to make the poor rise from the rubble to delight over the plight of the once-wealthy (v 4)a. The rich will be crying out "We're ruined" (v 4b) and the poor will be taunting them. It is a picture of complete reversal.

4. For whom would this judgment of a reversal of fortunes be:
• **bad news?** The wealthy and privileged who have (deliberately or unthinkingly) done well out of a system that pushes others down. This is a word of judgment to them.

• **a cause for rejoicing?** If you are poor, this is the dawn of a new day breaking on the horizon. This is a word of hope, not of judgment. To be poor is not automatically to be lazy or dependent, despite the stereotypes; but to be poor is, in most places and at most times, to be stuck without the ability to chase a dream or entertain realistic hope. If that were your life, then Micah 2 would be a breath of fresh air to you because it would be a shimmering hope in the distance. It would be a picture of power that you did not know you could ever have dreamed of. It would be a pointer to a God who does not oppress you, and will not stand to see you oppressed.
It is hard to read the Bible from that perspective if you have not experienced that life. But it is critical to seek to do so. (If we read these verses as verses of judgment to be concerned about, then likely we are those who have done well out of life, and who need to think hard about whether we are acting oppressively.)

5. How do those described in verses 1-2 respond to Micah's challenge (v 6)? They tell him to be quiet. These things are not for a prophet to preach about, they say—and they assert confidently that his warnings will not come to pass.

- **What would they rather hear (v 11)?** Micah was not written for those who want a comfortable low-stress life. But that is who Micah was speaking to: people who would rather hear easy lies than hard truths, who wanted to enjoy the good things of life—wine and strong drink—without too much thought about their conduct. **Why, do you think?** Because they wanted to hear their preachers say things that supported their lifestyle. It is always easier to hear preaching that agrees with what we already think and how we have already chosen to live; it's far harder to be willing to accept that we may have got something wrong and need to change. The people then (like us today) needed truth, but wanted comfort.

6. In what way does God follow rebuke with restoration [in v 12-13]? There is hope for those who truly are God's people—the "remnant." A Shepherd is on his way, who will gather his people together and give all of them "pasture"—all they need, for all of them (v 12). He will break through the breach—he will burst open the gates of oppression—to lead us to the dawn of a new day. And this Shepherd is no less than the King, the LORD God himself (v 13).

7. APPLY: What would the oppression in Micah's society look like in yours? Make sure you focus on your own society, and aim to think of specific ways that people may oppress deliberately (v 1), but also in more subtle, even often unnoticed, ones (v 2, 9).

- **How might you be guilty of it, either proactively or simply permissively?** This is the key, and uncomfortable, part of this question.
- **Read 2 Corinthians 8 v 9. How do we see in Christ the way to use our privileges rightly?** Jesus did not use his wealth for himself, but rather, gave it all for those who had nothing. Out of his poverty, he made us rich. He used everything he had in the service of others, undeserving though they were and are. Jesus came and effectively said, *I'm bringing in a new order; the last are first now; the poor are blessed; the oppressed are free.* How does he bring in this new order? *I will take the last spot myself,* he says. *Do you want riches? Make me poor. Do you want strength? Strip me of all of mine and make me weak.* And he is not only our Savior in doing this; he is also our model.

8. How does Micah say power is being used (or misused) by:
- **Israel's political rulers ([3] v 1-3, 9-11)?**
  - v 1: The question they are asked is rhetorical. It is Micah's way of saying: *You are the ones who are supposed to know about and secure justice, because you have the power to do so. But you haven't.*
  - v 2a: They hate good and love evil—they're using their positions in exactly the opposite way to how they should do.
  - v 2b-3: This is powerful imagery. The people they lead are seen simply as means to their own ends. Furthermore—and you'll need to explain this to your group—the Assyrians, the power in Micah's time, under the rule of Sennacherib, had a common practice: they captured their enemies and flayed their skin while they were still alive.

So God is basically saying, *I know that you're my national magistrates, but you are metaphorically doing to your own people what the enemy is doing to your people.* That is the worst indictment there can be: that the leaders of a people are acting as the enemies of the people.

- v 9-11: This is a conclusion and gives more detail. They detest justice and are crooked; they build at the expense of the health or lives of others (their "blood"); they are open to being bribed.

- **Israel's religious leaders (v 5, 11)?**
  - v 5: When these religious leaders receive money for the work they've been called to do, they then speak a warm, comforting message of peace to the people. But when they don't get the money, they preach war. Their prophecies can be bought. They use their power to line their pockets.
  - v 11: Again, while preaching safety complacently, assuming God must be on their side and teaching others to assume the same, they are using their positions for their own financial gain.

Here's a working definition of misused power: it is taking the influence God has given you for the sake of the common good and using it against others for selfish gain. And this is what the leaders of Israel were doing.

EXPLORE MORE
Read Mark 14 v 53-65; 15 v 1-15. How do we see both political and religious leaders abusing their power in the trial and sentencing of Jesus? The religious leaders are determined to convict Jesus, even if it requires an unjust trial (14 v 55-58). They envy Jesus' status and popularity (15 v 10), so they use their power to bring him down. Pilate, the Roman governor, allows a man he suspects is innocent to be sentenced

to death rather than using his power for good. He would rather please the crowd than do what is right. Here is injustice and self-serving use of power that leads to the shedding of innocent blood. It is exactly the kind of misuse of position and power that Micah describes in Micah 3.

⌄

- **How do we see the same misuse of power in our political systems and our religious institutions today? Why is it so tempting to misuse power in this way, do you think? What excuses do people make for it?**

9. What is God going to do in response to this (v 4, 6-7)? Verse 4: God says that he will not hear these religious leaders when they call out to him. God will not listen to them, because when the marginalized are in need of support from these leaders, they do not listen to them.

Verses 6-7 further describe the nature of this silence from God. God is saying, *You don't listen to the people who are weak and lack privilege. If, therefore, you are engaging in social injustice, why should I listen to your plea? And if you will not speak truth to those who need truth from you, why would you expect truth from me when you look for it? You chose to be silent when you should have spoken; you will find silence from me when you wish I would speak.*

When God withdraws his guidance and revelation, people are lost. And so the leaders of Israel will be too.

10. What does Micah do with the power that he has been given (v 8)? Micah is the inverse of the false prophets. He is somebody who is filled with power and the Spirit of God, and he is filled with justice and might. He is not filled with injustice, the abuse of power, or his own identity. Rather, he is filled with power that comes from the Spirit of the Lord—and he uses that power to pursue justice bravely, and declares the truth unsparingly.

- **Read Mark 10 v 42-45 and Philippians 2 v 6-8. How is Micah pointing us towards the Lord Jesus?** We see in Jesus the "ultimate Micah." He had all the power of the eternal Son of Man (read Daniel 7 v 13-14). He had the position of the second Person of the Trinity, deserving of the praise of all of heaven and earth. And he used that position and power to serve others, supremely in giving his life on the cross. Though he was the victim of flagrant abuse of power by both the religious and political leaders of his day, nevertheless he always used his greater power for the good of others. Compare Jesus with what Micah says of the leaders in Micah 3 v 9-10: "Hear this, you heads of the house of Jacob and rulers of the house of Israel, who detest justice and make crooked all that is straight, who build Zion with blood and Jerusalem with iniquity." Jesus built Zion and Jerusalem too, but not with the blood of others; he built with his own blood. He used his power in love.

11. APPLY: What would you say to someone who says, "Power corrupts, so as Christians we should shun power and influence"? This question is designed to help you discuss how we need to avoid two equal and opposite errors. The first is the one Micah is highlighting in his society—the selfish abuse of power. The second is the one the quote in this question is making—the refusal to use power at all.
God's people are called to be steward leaders. We are leaders because we

have power, rank, and privilege (to some degree)—but we are also stewards, using that power to bless others in God's world. Power does not corrupt if it is used in the service of Christ and according to the model of Christ. If we shun power or if we're timid about our power, that won't honor God because he has given us the gift of power and privilege, and he wants us to leverage it well. We are not to misuse it, but equally we are not to refuse to use it.

12. APPLY: "Have the same mindset as Christ Jesus" (Philippians 2 v 5, NIV). What positions do you have in the various areas of your life that mean you have some amount of power? Think about the coming week in terms of the power you will have in your work context, your living situation, your neighborhood, and your relationships with family and friends. We have all sorts of power and privilege.

- **What would it look like to use that power in a loving, Christ-like way?** Because we follow Jesus, we do not domineer, we do not oppress, and we do not live in superiority, but we are able to be humble and bold—to be steward leaders. As a result, we can reflect the beautiful, paradoxical leadership of this greatest King, who gave his life.

3 Micah 4 v 1-13
THE LONG ROAD TO RESTORATION

THE BIG IDEA
God will restore his people by bringing them to the place of his dwelling and rule—but the way there will not be easy, and will sometimes be painful.

SUMMARY
In Micah 4, in the midst of all the chaos that has been described in the first three chapters, God injects a vision of astounding hope. The idea of restoration is key here: God doesn't just discard and get rid of things. He renews them (e.g. swords turned into plowshares, v 3).

The opening verses set up the promise of restoration as focused on God's "mountain"—the place where he dwells and also the place where he rules. We then see a reversal of the portrayal of Israel's sin and God's judgment in chapters 1 – 3. God promises to restore twisted hearts to worship the one true God (4 v 2) and undo the damage of oppression (v 3). Both the lame (the pain caused by brokenness inside of us) and those who are cast off (the pain caused by the brokenness of circumstances outside of us) will experience renewal (v 6-7). But it's a "long road"—life before then will be painful (v 9-11). For those in Micah's day, restoration will come through the pain of defeat and Babylonian exile. The principle is: what you know to be true of the future will inform your experience now.

The same is true for us. Hebrews 12 v 22-24 shows that Jesus is the fulfillment of this promise of one who will rule and dwell from Jerusalem. He died at Calvary on the side of Mount Zion so that his people experience only the shadow of God's judgment for sin in the brokenness, fallenness, oppression and injustice of this life. When Jesus returns to fully establish his kingdom, the vision of Micah 4 will be fully and finally fulfilled.

OPTIONAL EXTRA
Junk modeling. In Micah 4 v 3, God promises to turn swords into plowshares—what can your group turn a pile of trash into? Split the group into smaller teams, and provide them with some tape and a bunch of old boxes, bottles, cartons, newspaper, foil, etc. Set a five- or ten-minute timer and see who can come up with the most imaginative creation!

GUIDANCE FOR QUESTIONS
1. How does our view of our future affect the way we live in the present?
If your group are struggling, ask them to imagine having a very difficult day towards the end of May. How would their perspective be changed if they knew they had a two-week vacation in a wonderful location, starting three weeks later? How would it be changed if they knew they had no vacation at all coming up?

- **What difference would it make when you face a problem now:**
  - **if you knew it would be solved by tomorrow?**
  - **if you knew that things were only going to get worse, for decades?**
Again, the point is to realize just how

much our view of the present, and our reactions and emotions in our present, is informed by the way we are viewing our future. You'll return to this after Q7.

2. Out of 10, how hopeful and joy-filled has Micah 1 – 3 been? A low score! There have been some glimmers of hope, but not many. Surely no one in your group will score it higher than a 3!

3. How does Micah's tone change in these verses? There is a hopeful shift in gears here. Suddenly the tone is one of hope, of joy, of confidence.

4. What will "the mountain of the house of the LORD" be like (v 1-2)? When the Bible talks about mountains, it's not just a geographic reference or a beautiful image; there are deep theological implications for what the biblical writers are trying to say when they make reference to a mountain. Mountains are where God rules through his law (Exodus 19 – 31) and where God dwells (Mount Zion was the mountain on the side of which Jerusalem was built, and therefore where God's temple was situated). Verse 2 makes this clear—going to Mount Zion means going to God's house, and from Zion goes "the law." And the people will want to be taught so they can walk God's way (v 2). So these verses are full of hope because they are based on the future reality when God's place and God's law will be pre-eminent— God's mountain shall be "the highest of the mountains." The promise of restoration involves both his presence and his rule. God promises to come to his people and, in doing so, to make all things right.

5. How does the restoration pictured in verses 1-4 reverse the portrayal of Israel's sin and God's judgment in

chapters 1 – 3? Compare these verses:
- 1 v 3: "The LORD … will … tread upon the high places" and 4 v 2: "the house of the LORD shall be established as the highest of the mountains."
- 1 v 4: "The mountains will melt under him" and 4 v 1: "The mountain of the house of the LORD shall be established."
- 1 v 7: "Carved images shall be beaten to pieces" and 4 v 3: "They shall beat their swords into plowshares."

The land described in chapters 1 – 3 is rife with idolatry, leading to injustice, violence and oppression, which will result in defeat and exile. In 4 v 3-4, God comes as judge, there is peace among the nations (who stream to Mount Zion), and everyone has their own vine and fig tree (no one is oppressing anyone else). There is nothing to fear.

6. Read Hebrews 12 v 22. How does the writer to the Hebrews link Micah's vision to our faith as Christians? The writer to the Hebrews uses an image very like the one of Micah 4 v 1-5. He is saying that Mount Zion is a reference to, a shadow of, Jesus. Jesus is the fulfillment of the promise made about how God would rule and dwell from Jerusalem and give to his people the law and the word. His rule and dwelling are now fulfilled in Jesus. And when Jesus returns to fully establish his kingdom, the vision of v 3-4 will be fully, finally fulfilled. As Christians, we experience the glory of Mount Zion now through and in faith in Christ; and we walk confidently towards the eventual full experience of it, when our King returns to rule.

7. APPLY: What would change in how you view your life today if you had a clearer view of your restored future? What you know of your future will inform the way you endure all the suffering, oppression, and injustice of this life, to whatever degree you experience those things. We will be able to endure if we know that God has already, in Jesus, brought about restoration, and so he is restoring us now in all the circumstances of our lives (Romans 8 v 28), and he will one day fully restore us. We will be able to experience all of the harsh conditions of the dungeon while we're living here on earth with the knowledge that the promise-maker is also the one who is a promise-keeper.

- **How will you help remind each other of the heaven-on-earth Mount Zion that Hebrews 12 v 22?** Make sure you're practical. One group member, for example, may struggle in a particular circumstance or at a particular time each week, and a simple text would suffice to lift their gaze back to their King and his kingdom.

8. What will happen to weakness and suffering (v 6-7)? There are two groups of people who are being addressed: the lame (the pain caused by brokenness inside of us) and those who are cast off (the pain caused by the brokenness of circumstances outside of us). Whether our pain comes from inside or outside, God promises to restore us from that pain. All pain will be a thing of the past one day.

9. What will life be like before then for God's people (v 9-11)? Painful. God compares his people's experience to "a woman in labor" (v 9, 10). V 10 prophesies the exile of Judah to Babylon—the people will be restored, but God will redeem them "there" (v 10). He says, *You're going to go through pain, because you're going to go into exile. There will be suffering, but I'm not ultimately going to leave you there; restoration is going to come through that.*

10. What will Israel need to remember, which the nations "do not know" (v 12-13, see also v 8)?
- That the LORD God has a plan (v 12), and that even the strongest nation and people are mere "sheaves" on his "threshing floor." The nations may live as though the LORD is not real or cannot help; but his people must remember that nothing is outside his purposes.
- That the LORD God will triumph, and his people with him (v 13). They will know the pain of defeat by their enemies, but then beyond that they will know the joy of victory.
- v 8: Restoration will come through kingship. God is promising a return to the highest points of the history of God's people through the coming of "kingship for the daughter of Jerusalem."

EXPLORE MORE
What will come to Zion, which means that God's time of restoration has arrived (v 8)? A King.
Read Luke 1 v 32-33. When did that time of restoration begin? With the birth of Jesus—he is the one who comes to reign "over the house of Jacob forever."
How does what Micah says about the restoration make the announcement of the incarnation to Mary even more exciting? It is hard, living this side of the incarnation, cross, and resurrection, to appreciate the burden of the wait for God's promises to be fulfilled. Gabriel's announcements to Mary, and just previously to her relative Elizabeth, ended four centuries of heaven's silence. But now here, at last, was the King, coming to Israel to restore Israel. Here, at last, was the One in whom all of Israel's hopes were (or should have been) placed. It is no wonder that both Zechariah and Mary broke into songs of

praise, because God had now moved to fulfil his promises (1 v 54-55, 68-75).

11. APPLY: What perspective on present suffering are these verses teaching God's people? We'll get up each morning giving thanks to God, and go on doing so throughout the day, whatever the day brings our way. We'll wake up knowing there's a purpose and meaning for each aspect of our life—the good and bad, the chosen and unchosen. Rather than saying, "Woe is me!" and rather than being anxious, we'll live with hope, knowing that restoration lies beyond our pain and comes through our pain. Pain and suffering are not signs of the absence of God. They are a place in which to experience the presence of God because he will restore us through them.

- **Read Romans 5 v 2-5 and James 1 v 12. In what way do these passages reflect and extend what we read in Micah 4?**
  - Romans 5 v 2-5: Because we have "hope of the glory of God" (i.e. a certain knowledge that we will one day stand in God's perfect presence) we "rejoice in our sufferings." Further, we know that God will not only restore us beyond pain, but he will work in us through our pain, producing endurance, character, and increasing hope. So God will not evacuate us from difficult circumstances, but lead us through them to teach us. This is the message of Micah 4 on an individual level, and Paul is able to add that God is dwelling in us by his Spirit to assure us of his love for us during those painful times (v 5).
  - James 1 v 12: Again, we see restoration beyond "trial." As we remain steadfast, we look forward to the crown of life.
- **What comfort do you tend to offer other Christians when they are in pain**

(whether due to circumstances or due to the consequences of sin)? Do these passages reshape your response in any way? Think about what we may say that reflects more of the Western world's view of pain than the Bible's. E.g. we may react as though a time of trial is a disaster, and promise simply to pray that the Lord would remove it. We may seek to offer clichéd, untrue phrases (like "I'm sure it will get better soon") or hope that is not built on confidence in God ("You're due a break" or "Things will all work out in the end"). Micah 4 teaches us to acknowledge the pain, and to remind each other that suffering is a normal part of the Christian life, and to pray for restoration beyond and through the pain, and for God to be forming our characters through the pain.

12. APPLY: Read Luke 23 v 33-46. What had to happen on Mount Zion in order for us to be able to look towards the restored heaven-on-earth Mount Zion? Remember, Micah 4 is a picture of the restored Mount Zion: a kingdom begun in the coming of Jesus and that will be finally established upon his return. But when the King came to Mount Zion, and to the city of Jerusalem, built on its side, he did not sit on a throne, but rather, died on a cross. The cross is where "the house of the LORD"—the presence of God in human form—was "lifted up" (Micah 4 v 1). He was insulted and rejected. He experienced the judgment of ultimate exile from relationship with his Father. That is how he restores us. On the cross, he experienced the exile of separation from God's blessing and loving presence that you and I deserve, so that we might receive the homecoming that Jesus deserved. This is how we know that restoration from pain is utterly and ultimately certain.

4 Micah 5 v 1-15
HE WILL SHEPHERD HIS FLOCK

THE BIG IDEA
God himself comes to his people as our shepherd, to rescue, lead, and change us. We need to give up our self-sufficiency, ask him to help us do this, and enjoy following him.

SUMMARY
Chapter 4 promised restoration for God's people; the first part of chapter 5 focuses on what the restorer will be like. He will be divine ("from old," 5 v 2), yet also have a "birth" (v 3)—and in a surprising small town such as Bethlehem (v 2)! He will be a strong and majestic shepherd who brings peace (v 4-5). Of course, we find all these words fulfilled in Christ (see John 10 v 14).

Although the Israelites are heading for invasion (Micah 5 v 5-6)—and beyond that, exile—God promises that one day a "remnant" of his people will overcome their enemies (v 7-9). It is not just their external enemies who will be cut off but all the idols that ensnare them and distract them from depending on the Lord (v 10-14).

This study will call your group to abandon attempts at self-sufficiency and come to depend on the Lord Jesus as their shepherd. Because Jesus received the rejection that we deserved, he achieved the rescue that we desperately need. He alone is our Rescuer. Israel needed to learn that; so do we.

OPTIONAL EXTRA
Cup stack challenge. Make a "grabber" by tying four pieces of string to an elastic band. Set out six plastic cups on a table. Challenge one group member to stack the cups in a pyramid using only the grabber, by pulling on the string to stretch and contract the elastic band. This should be difficult! Then invite two people to do it together—this should be much easier. Use this game as a fun way to introduce the ideas of self-sufficiency and depending on another.

GUIDANCE FOR QUESTIONS
1. Why is self-sufficiency so attractive? Why do we aspire to be, and seek to appear as, self-made successes? Because it means we can feel in control and comfortable, and feel that we have achieved this state ourselves. It means we can feel that we have life figured out. Also, we live in a culture that prizes self-sufficiency and self-autonomy. Many of us like self-made people. We like successful entrepreneurs. We like pioneers. We like trailblazers. We laud people who seem to have it all together and appear to have done it all themselves.

2. How does verse 1 describe the hopelessness of Israel's situation? Verse 1 is describing what will happen when the Assyrian king, Sennacherib, launches his campaign against Judah (see 1 v 15-16). The Assyrians occupied the whole land, right up to the walls of Jerusalem (see 2 Kings 18). "O daughter of troops" seems to be a way of describing their weakness and inability to fight back and protect their land and people. God has a strong sense of what's going on. He knows. He's not far off and distant. There will not be a whole army of troops fighting for Judah, but only "a daughter" of troops remaining.

Micah also foretells the powerlessness of Hezekiah, the king of Judah, who will be completely at the power of the Assyrian empire. The enemy will come so close to the king that they will be able to strike him on the cheek. This is an act that will bring great shame to him. He will be defenseless as the attacks come.

3. What do verses 2-3 reveal about the identity of Israel's rescuer?

(1) *He will come from a surprising place (v 2).* Bethlehem was such a small town that it wasn't even listed by Joshua when he was looking at all the 150 towns and cities that were in the area. No one would expect a rescuer to come from such a small, weak place. But of course, Bethlehem is also the place from where David, the great shepherd-become-king, came from (1 Samuel 16).

(2) *He is "from of old" (v 2).* The word here for "old" is used only two other times in the Old Testament—once in Habakkuk 1 and once in Deuteronomy 33. In both instances, the word is used as an adjective to describe God. In Habakkuk 1 v 12 it says, "Are you not from everlasting [or "of old"], O LORD my God, my Holy One?" Deuteronomy 33 v 27 speaks of, "The eternal [or "of old"] God." Here in Micah it's describing the restorer who will come in the future.

⊌

- [If your group doesn't pick up on the significance of the coming one being "of old"] The word here for "of old" is used only two other times in the Old Testament. Read Deuteronomy 33 v 27 (where the word is translated "eternal") and Habakkuk 1 v 12 (where it is rendered "everlasting"). What is startling about Micah's announcement that the coming ruler's "coming forth is from of old" (Micah 5 v 2)?

(3) *He will be born (v 3).* This would be unremarkable were it not for the announcement in verse 2 that he is divine— "of old." The divine restorer will come as a baby, born to a woman in the normal way, entering the world to the cries of labor. Jesus' mother Mary had a child who was older than she was. His origins were of old, from ancient days. She and Joseph had authority as his parents but he had authority as their eternal God.

4. How is this ruler described in verses 4-5a? The category God chooses to use to describe his coming ruler is that of "shepherd"—a shepherd who will rule in the name and majesty of God. He is a gentle shepherd who is going to provide for the needs of the flock, but at the same time he will come in the name and majesty of the great God, and his rule will cover the earth, so that for his people, he will "be their peace" (v 5). So the shepherd is humble, but he is also almighty.

- **In what sense is this the kind of leader that all people need?** Deep within our hearts we all long for a shepherd to come and take care of our needs. If and when we have problems, we want to know if there is anyone out there who is able to take care of us. Is there someone out there who is going to make everything right? Is there someone who is going to exercise control in the midst of all my chaos?

5. Jesus described himself as "the good shepherd" (John 10 v 14). How does Micah 5 show us something of what he meant? He was saying that he is gentle,

and that he cares—and also that he is all-powerful, and that he leads. He can offer victory and security and peace. He will rule with gentleness, but he will rule. In the end, what God is asking and requiring of his people is not perfection, but submission; he does not call us to be flawless, but to follow.

6. APPLY: In what different ways do people reveal their deep-down longing for a "good shepherd"? Follow people's anger and you will often find that they have been let down by someone (a spouse, leader, child, boss) whom they were treating as their shepherd, to usher them into the life they were searching for. Follow people's source of anxiety and you will often find a yearning for a shepherd too. Equally, the reasons for despair lead in a similar direction.

7. APPLY: In what ways does self-sufficiency get in the way of enjoying having Jesus as our shepherd? Self-sufficiency tells us that we don't need a shepherd for we can be our own shepherd—or that we can control another shepherd in order to gain what we need. So (for example) we seek to encourage or berate or manipulate our spouse into being the perfect spouse, to achieve the life we want. Self-sufficiency prevents us from giving up control. So then we will not listen to Jesus as our shepherd, and instead of following where he leads and trusting in his provision, when things get hard or confusing we will say, *Hang on, Jesus. I think I will do this my way. I think I know better right now.* But self-sufficiency won't bring us what we need.

8. But what else does God promise to do with his people?
- **v 7:** Note: The word "remnant" is not talking about the special, good people.

The word is simply used to refer to God's people—sinners whom God has saved. This remnant is not some separate group who need to keep themselves withdrawn from everyone else: "The remnant of Jacob shall be in the midst of many peoples." God's people are going to live among them as dew, or showers. This is an agricultural metaphor to refer to the blessings of God. The Middle East was an arid place, so having any form of water was a blessing. God's people are called to be a blessing and to benefit those who are around them—their neighbors, their society, and their community.

- **v 8-9:** At the same time as using his people to bless those around them, God will also give them victory over those around them who oppress them, so that there can be peace. The Assyrian will have a day of treading over God's people (v 5-6). But there will be a time in the future, in a period when the Shepherd-Ruler will come (v 2), where the remnant, the people of God, will do the treading (v 8). The people of God have been called to be a blessing to others but also have been promised that they will prevail over those others who seek to crush them.

9. What will God "cut off" or "root out" (v 10-14)? How would each be something that the Israelites could look to for self-sufficient independence?
- Their military power and their ability to fight for themselves. "I will cut off your horses from among you and will destroy your chariots" (v 10).
- Their places of retreat and refuge. "I will cut off the cities of your land and throw down all your strongholds" (v 11). Cities represented safety.
- Their attempt to control the future. "I will cut off sorceries from your hand, you shall

have no more tellers of fortunes" (v 12). Sorcery offered control—security.

- All of their idols—God will separate them from allegiances with false gods, and to help and rescue them. "I will cut off your carved images and your pillars from among you, and you shall bow down no more to the work of your hands; and I will root out your Asherah images from among you and destroy your cities" (v 13-14). These are the pagan foreign gods, Baal and Asherah, who offered harvest and fertility.

EXPLORE MORE
How did each of these individuals need to give up any pretense to self-sufficiency in order to come to the good shepherd? And what did they gain from him when they did?

- **Mark 2 v 13-15:** Levi must leave his means of acquiring wealth. He follows Jesus, finds himself the center of a banquet—and is renamed Matthew, follows Jesus through his life, witnesses his resurrection, and writes a Gospel.
- **Mark 5 v 21-43 (there are two individuals in view here)** The bleeding woman needs to run out of options—she has to be desperate to risk humiliation and disappointment. But in reaching out, she finds herself healed. And in fact, Jesus calls her to more than she has hoped for, for she finds herself being spoken to by him, and hearing him assure her of her salvation, through faith.

  Jairus has to give up any idea that his position as a synagogue ruler means he can rely on himself or his own means. He has to come to Jesus and beg for help. Then he has to wait, learning that even his own plans and timings need to be placed under Jesus' authority. But he sees his daughter raised from the dead.
- **Mark 10 v 17-22** This is a "trick

question"—for here is a man who refuses to give up his sense of sufficiency in his reliance on his wealth. And because he will not do that, he misses out on the joy of following Jesus. He cannot both feel self-sufficient and follow Christ. Sadly, he chooses the former.

10. APPLY: To what do we look for self-sufficiency? Think about the reasons for those things that God told his people he would "cut off," and ask yourselves:
1. What do you look to for your power? Where do you find your strength and resolve?
2. What do you look to for security? Where is your refuge?
3. How do you attempt to control your future? What do you worry about in your future? Which decisions cause you stress because you feel that on their outcome hangs your future happiness?
4. What family set-up are you looking to for happiness or confidence? Who in your life do you "need" in order for things to be OK? Or: What sexual experience do you feel you need in order to be "whole"?

11. APPLY: What would it look like for you to allow God to "cut off" those things, so that you can follow the good shepherd? Obviously, your answers here will depend on your answers to Q9. Encourage your group to see that it would be better for these things to be "cut off" than to end up worshiping them rather than Jesus. Perhaps share ways you can, by looking back, see that God removed good things so you would not become reliant on them. Having identified in Q9 your idols, which you look to in order to remain independent from Christ, consider what it would look like to put them away and rely on Jesus and obey him in those areas.

5 Micah 6 v 1-16
FINDING JUSTICE

THE BIG IDEA
God requires us proactively to pursue justice and kindness in all we do. In his saving acts, God himself is the great example of doing justice and acting kindly, and this is our motivation to live this way in response.

SUMMARY
The main theme of Micah 6 is justice, and this whole chapter reads like a court scene. First, God summons the court of his creation and names the defendants—his people Israel (v 1-2). The implied "indictment" is all the charges that have already been set out in chapters 1 – 3: complete lack of regard for the weak and poor (chapter 2) and rampant misuse of power on all levels of society (chapter 3)—all driven by misshapen, idolatrous desires (chapter 1).

Next, God sets the standard of what he requires. Religious sacrifices mean nothing (6 v 6-7) if his people do not "do justice," "love kindness," and "walk humbly with" him (v 8). In many ways, verse 8 is key to the whole book of Micah, and we will spend much of this study unpacking it and exploring its implications.

Then follows the charge and verdict (v 9-12): God's people are guilty of getting rich unjustly, using manipulative weights and measures, and using violence and deceit.

In verses 13-16, God delivers the sentence: First, they will not receive or enjoy all that they are chasing in their calculating, manipulative, self-focused way of life (v 14-15). Finally, they will be exiled (v 16).

Although the verdict in this passage is damning, when we read it in the context

of the whole Bible story there is still hope. Just as God's people in Micah's time could look back on the exodus as proof of God's unrelenting loving kindness (v 3-5), so Christians today can look back at the cross—God's own Son standing "in the dock" in our place—as even greater proof (2 Corinthians 5 v 21; Romans 8 v 1). The gospel is what shows us God's justice and kindness, and it is also what frees and motivates us to live in this way that God requires and is pleased by.

OPTIONAL EXTRA
To help your group really apply this passage (Q7), do some research beforehand so that you can suggest something practical that your group could do together to "do justice" in your community. Is there a local charity or project you could volunteer for? A petition or campaign you could support? A cause that you could organize a special prayer meeting for? Of course, the application of this passage is much broader than this—but you've got to start somewhere. Who knows what it might grow into?

GUIDANCE FOR QUESTIONS
1. What is justice? When we think of doing justice, we typically think of something like performing retribution. Most people equate justice with punishing wrongs. Therefore, justice is something that the state enacts, not something that is a personal call on our lives. That's certainly part of what justice entails, but it's actually much broader than that—as we'll see.

2. What does God tell his people to remember (v 4-5)? The bedrock event in Israel's history—the exodus from Egypt and the journey through the wilderness, to the land God had promised them. For centuries, God's people had lived under the oppressive yoke of the Egyptian regime. But God raised up leaders like Moses, Aaron, and Miriam to free them from oppression. As they were going to that place, from Shittim to Gilgal (v 5), God's people were assaulted again, in particular by a king of Moab named Balak (Numbers 22). God raised up a prophet, Balaam, and a talking donkey to thwart the Moabite forces and to protect his people (Numbers 22 – 24). *Remember this,* says God.

• **So what is the answer to his questions in verse 3?** God had done nothing bad to his people, and everything that was kind. He didn't do anything to weary them—in fact, they were the ones who had been wearisome. But despite everything the LORD had done for them, by Micah's time God's people were effectively telling him, *Man, we wish you weren't around here anymore. Why be so demanding?*

3. What controversial possibility does Micah raise in verses 6-7? That God is not pleased with overflowing sacrificial offerings. Micah says that you can bring burnt offerings—for a Jew at this time, these would have been the most costly, because all the other offerings allowed for taking a portion home to eat, but the whole of a burnt offering was given to the fire. Micah says you can take the things that are the best, the cream of the crop: calves a year old, thousands of rams, rivers of oil, your firstborn child… but you must still question whether God is actually pleased with this.

• **Read Amos 5 v 21-24. What is the answer to God's questions in Micah 6 v 6-7?** God is not pleased. In fact he hates religious ritual and effort and will not accept it if it is not accompanied by "justice" and "righteousness" (v 24). In our terms, you can do church until you're blue in the face, but it's all a sham if it doesn't crystallize as concrete love for your neighbors. That's the point here, and in Micah 6.

4. What has God said is "good" (Micah 6 v 8)?
• Do justice
• Love kindness
• Walk humbly with your God

In your own words, what do you think each of these three requirements means?
• *Justice:* Certainly this includes giving perpetrators their due, but doing justice is also giving those who cannot stand up for themselves—the victims, the poor, the powerless, the vulnerable, the voiceless—their due as well. It is more than only punishing wrong; it is creating a situation and a society where everything is right—a society where every last person in it, including the most vulnerable and the weakest, can flourish and thrive. That's what doing justice, according to the Bible, really means.
• *Kindness:* Explain to your group that the word Micah uses for "kindness" (*hesed*) could also be translated as unqualified love, limitless love, and stubborn, unceasing, dogged love. So kindness is to say, "I refuse to give up on you, even if everyone else tells me that I should. I will not budge in my loyalty to you. I will stay with you even in the moments when there's nothing in it for me."
• *Walk humbly with your God*: This means to allow God to call the tune, to set the

path for our life and conduct. It is to be humble enough to listen to him tell us that what counts is not only "worship activity" but also to do justice and love kindness; to allow him to tell us what pleases him, rather than tell him what we think he ought to be pleased about.

EXPLORE MORE
Read Matthew 23 v 23-25. To whom is Jesus speaking here? "Scribes and Pharisees"—in other words, men who take their religion very seriously and know their Scriptures very well.
How is he making the same point as Micah did? They are very good at tithing carefully. But they have neglected "the weightier matters" of how God calls his people to live—namely, "justice and mercy and faithfulness." So they seem religious, and assume God is pleased with them—but in fact the Son of God issues a word of condemnatory judgment to them—"woe" (v 23). Their outward religious commitment is a cover for their "greed and self-indulgence" (v 25). They are just the same as their ancestors in Micah's day.
How does this make Micah 6 more challenging for us as professing worshipers of God today? The attitude and behavior Micah describes is something that is a danger for "religious people" in all times and places. It was not only a problem in his time. It was around in Jesus' day, too. And we have no reason to think that we are immune today. It is possible for us to turn up to church on a Sunday, read our Bibles each day, give a tenth of our income, attend our church prayer meeting… and not be pleasing God. Indeed, it is possible to do all these things and still hear Jesus say to us, "Woe to you."

5. How had God already exemplified to

his people a passion to "do justice and to love kindness" (v 4-5)? By rescuing his people when they could not stand up for themselves and leading them to a land where, under his law, everything would be right, the vulnerable would be protected and all could flourish; by refusing to leave his people whatever happened, by showering them with unconditional, ever-flowing love. Micah is trying to grab the hearts of his people and say, *Do you remember that love that means that I looked on you and cared for you and redeemed you and blessed you, not because you deserved it, but because I loved you* (see Deuteronomy 7 v 7-8). *Remember that love.*

6. APPLY: How might we as the church today make the same mistake that the people had in Micah's day, do you think? You will likely have already discussed this as you have studied the passage, but it is crucial to realize that we can fall into the same trap as the people in Micah's day. Micah says, in the language of today, that you can give everything that means anything; your time, your money, your possessions, your goods, but you must not assume this means God is pleased with you. How easy it is to select particular religious activities to mask neglect of the harder call to do justice and love kindness.

7. APPLY: What would it look like for you to "do justice, and to love kindness":
• **within your church?**
• **in your workplace?**
• **in your family?**
• **in your community?**
Remind your group of the definitions of justice and kindness (see answer to Q4 above). Encourage them to be specific in terms of their answers to this question. (You

may like to give time to write answers down before sharing and discussing them). Four areas of life are highlighted but you may like to choose two to think about carefully, which is better than rushing through all four.

8. What is the content of the charges?

- **v 10:** There is the possession of unjustly procured treasures. The people were involved in procuring treasures for themselves in unrighteous ways. God cannot forget or overlook these injustices. To do so would be to a de facto means of blessing them and making himself complicit in the injustice.
- **v 11:** Using manipulative weights and measures. In the ancient world, standardized measures were hard to establish, so trading was done on an honor system where people would use just weights and measures. These people were using unjust measures and weights. They were circumventing the honor system and deceitfully manipulating people's trust as they were engaged in commerce.
- **v 12:** An underlying web of violence and deceit. They were essentially doing anything for personal gain, even if it meant adopting deceitful ways or hurting people in the process. They weren't concerned about that because ultimately their priority was personal gain.
- **What are the modern-day equivalents of these sins?** It is absolutely key to help your group challenge their tendency to read passages like this and subconsciously think, "OK, but I don't do this. My scales work fine!"

So we need to think about what is going on here. The sin is to manipulate our financial power—or our professional position, or our relationships or even religion—for personal gain. Surely we are guilty of this. We often see all of life in economic and transactional terms. Because we are brought up in a society that tells us we are consumers, we look at all of life through a commercial lens. We see our lives by looking at the ways we can get the greatest benefit with the smallest amount of (financial, relational, time, etc) investment. The focus is on a self-derived gain, not on an other-oriented equality and justice. This, of course, has been the charge against the Israelites all along in the book of Micah.

You might like to discuss how we choose our careers, or chase a promotion, or select where we will live, as examples of where we easily fall into the trap of manipulating others in order to benefit ourselves. Give your group time to think individually about the Getting Personal after this question in the Study Guide.

9. What does verse 16 suggest is at the root of all this injustice and sin? Omri
and Ahab were kings of Israel who led the people into idol-worship (see 1 Kings 16 v 21 – 22 v 40). It all comes back to idolatry. The people have been following the counsel of the idolaters rather than listening to God's call to walk with him, love him, and pursue justice.

10. What is the sentence on this behavior ([Micah 6] v 13-16)? First, they
will not receive or enjoy all that they are chasing in their calculating, manipulative, self-focused way of life. They will eat without finding satisfaction or ending their hunger; they will save, but lose what they preserved (v 14). God will not give them what they trampled on others in order to get. God is saying in verse 15, *I will ensure that you are laboring in vain. You're not going to be able to find the joy and happiness of the work that you're*

involved in. I will not allow you to make this approach to life work well for you.

Second, they will finally be exiled (v 16). They will be separated from all they have worked to gain. They will leave it all behind. God will "make [them] a desolation."

☑

• **How do we see this dynamic of judgment in life in general, and not just on Israel then?** God does not allow our idols to satisfy. Often, people do get brought to justice in this life for dishonesty and injustice; but even if they do not, the dynamic of this world is that, in its fallen state, people find that the path they have chosen brings insecurity and unfulfillment rather than the riches and happiness they thought it would.

Furthermore, of course we are all finally exiled, for the ultimate exile is death. Death forces us to leave everything behind and separates us from all we have accumulated. It is why those who lay up stores in barns but are not rich toward God are, in Jesus' estimation, "fools" (Luke 12 v 13-21). One day, we will all have to stand under judgment.

11. Read 2 Corinthians 5 v 21 and Romans 8 v 1. What position does Jesus take in this divine courtroom, and what are the implications for his people?
God's own Son stood in the place of his accused and guilty people. He bore God's justice against our injustice. He became sin—became *our* sin. That means that the ultimate verdict has been given, and it is that someone has been exiled, struck, made desolate as he bore the sins of our self-gain. The ultimate verdict is that because Jesus went through this and bore our sentence, "there is therefore now no condemnation for those who are in Christ Jesus" (Romans 8 v 1).

12. APPLY: Read Philippians 3 v 7-9. What difference does knowing this make to us?
• **What will this mean for us in the way we view our lives day by day?**
We are who we are because of what Jesus Christ has done on our behalf. He has borne our sins in himself; he stood in our place so that we can get this declaration of being not guilty and completely innocent. This leads to a life that is free: one that pursues the gain of others and glorifies God; a life that is lived for his cause, and is not concerned about our ability or self-gain. Paul's life was restructured and reorganized in a completely different way, since death no longer meant losing everything but gaining everything. And so "whatever gain I had, I counted as loss for the sake of Christ ... for his sake ... I count [or, we might say, calculate] them as rubbish, in order that I may gain Christ and be found in him." This is the absolute opposite of what drove Israel in Micah's day, and what naturally drives us in ours. The gospel is what shows us God's justice and kindness (just as the exodus did for Israel), and it is also what frees and motivates us to live in this way that God requires and is pleased by.

6 Micah 7 v 1-20
WHO IS LIKE GOD?

THE BIG IDEA
Because God sent his Son to bear his people's punishment, we can lament the difficulties of this life freely and confidently, knowing that we are forgiven, that we will be heard, and that God will restore us. The Bible permits and encourages hope-filled lament.

SUMMARY
The first three words of chapter 7 ("Woe is me!") signal that this is the beginning of a lament. Lament expresses a state of intense emptiness and grief at the reality of life. The cause of Micah's lament is the disappearance of righteousness (7 v 2), the corruption of leaders (v 3-4), and the tearing of the social fabric (v 5-6). Yet Micah's lament results not in complacency or despair but in hope in God: he looks, he waits, and he trusts (v 7).

The next section points first to God's judgment on his people (v 9). Israel had already fallen in 722 BC, and they were brought into captivity under the Assyrian rule. The southern kingdom of Judah would fall to Babylon in 587 BC. But here God says that this would not be the end of the story, either for his people or for their enemies. Verses 11-17 paint a glorious picture of restoration beyond judgment. The other nations will be in awe of Israel as well, just as they were "in the days of old" (v 14), "when you came out of the land of Egypt" (v 15). Those who caused Israel to quake will find that now "they shall be in fear of [Israel]" (v 17). At the same time, though, God promises that "the boundary shall be far extended" (v 11). There will be a

remnant of God's inheritance that will even come from those enemy nations, not only from the nation of Israel (v 12).

Yet the climactic lines in verses 18-19 encapsulate one of the great tensions of Scripture. How can the God of *judgment* upon iniquity also be the God who *pardons* iniquity?

It's a tension we see ultimately resolved in Christ. He is the one who took our place and bore our punishment, "so that [God] might be just and the justifier of the one who has faith in Jesus" (Romans 3 v 26).

The hope-filled heart of the conclusion to Micah is this: vindicating justice is coming to, and for, God's people. God is not ultimately going to overlook their sin (v 9), yet the remnant of his inheritance—those who have been the recipients (as well as perpetrators) of unjust acts, oppression, idolatry, and the misuse of power—will be raised up in a way that does not undermine the justice of God. God has plans for his people beyond judgment.

OPTIONAL EXTRA
Before answering Q13, recap the whole book of Micah by watching The Bible Project's animated video summary entitled "Read Scripture: Micah" (youtu.be/MFEUEcylwLc).

GUIDANCE FOR QUESTIONS
1. In what ways do people react to huge setbacks or great difficulties?
• Anger
• Denial
• Despair

- Determination
- Indifference (when it is happening to those far away, or even around us)
- Anxiety
- Prayer
- Wailing
- Escaping

(This is not an exhaustive list!)

- **Do you think there are better and worse ways to react?** Allow your group to consider this question, but guide them to the conclusion that there are certainly some ways that are worse than others e.g. despair, indifference, anger are worse than determination (albeit this may be self-reliant) and prayer.

2. What is Micah reacting to (v 2-6)?

- v 2: The disappearance of righteousness. When he said in verse 1 that he found "no first-ripe fig that my soul desires," it turns out that Micah was speaking about the godly and the righteous in that way. He was saying that good fruit—righteousness—was nowhere for him to enjoy. Micah uses a very strange image of people hunting one another with a net (v 2). It simply shows that some people prey upon other people. They want to subdue other people for personal gain. Notice that the lack of knowledge of God is witnessed in community breakdown.
- v 3-4: The corruption of leaders and peace-keeping structures. God has given princes, judges, and "the great man" responsibility to steward their authority in order to care for the people whom God has entrusted into their hands. They're asked to weave peace into the structure of the community. They're supposed to be peace-weavers, weavers of shalom, but they have become obstructers of justice. What they weave together is evil, and they do it well. The best of the leaders is a thorn hedge (v 4).

- v 5-6: The tearing of the social fabric. Neighbors cannot be trusted, friends are unworthy of confidence, and family life is no better: spouses are emotionally estranged from one another, sons line up against fathers, daughters rebel against their mothers. Every man and every woman is for himself or herself.

3. How would you describe his reaction (v 1)? "Woe is me!" *What misery is mine!*

"Woe is me" is one of the most powerful, deeply-felt phrases that can be invoked. It sums up the feeling of a grieving mother who has lost a child, or a widower facing their spouse's funeral, or a conquered nation. "Woe is me!" is only used in the most dire, grim, ruinous circumstances. This is not self-pity—it is a right reaction of grief and overwhelming sadness at the reality of life. Micah does not deny what he sees, nor does he seek to look on the bright side. He is not indifferent. He stares it in the face and he lets it affect him.

4. APPLY: Why is it encouraging to know that the Bible permits—even encourages—lamenting? Because we

know that human experience is sometimes about singing, and it's sometimes about crying. The Bible deals with real life. Christianity does not ignore the wounds of the world; it draws near to them. It acknowledges suffering and pain. God created a world of *shalom*; it is a matter of grief that that is not the world we currently see. If we will not weep over it, we shall never really know the joy of the prospect of its restoration when its Master returns.

- **In what way do you, or your church, need to hear this permission and encouragement?** Modern Western Christianity has a difficulty understanding and appreciating the discipline of lament. Often we give the impression in our churches that only happy people can be Christians, so that we hide those things about which we need to lament. And individually, our pride can prevent us from being open about those things that we are struggling with; or we don't share them because we feel we are letting others down, or we fear they will not lament with us, but instead won't know what to do or will say unhelpful, sub-biblical things (e.g. "It will get better soon" or "It's not as bad as you think"). So obviously your answer here will depend on your own church and your group's circumstances—but it's likely you will need to think through whether you allow yourselves to lament, and how you respond to others when they lament.

5. APPLY: What causes you to say (or think) "Woe is me"? How does that match up with the reasons for Micah's lament here?
• **Is there anything that needs to change in your own priorities in life?** When we are honest, we realize that so much of our lamenting concerns only ourselves and our thwarted dreams or desires; at best, it may extend to the interests of our household. But when was the last time you lamented over the lack of godliness around you; or the corruption in the leaders over you; or the tearing of social fabric in your community? All too often we are indifferent when it comes to these things. We should not be.

6. What three things does Micah do in addition to his lament? Fundamentally, he hopes in his lament. We can break verse 7 into three actions: he looks, he waits, and then he trusts. He acknowledges that only God can help—that it will need divine

intervention to reverse what is happening. He accepts that God's timing is not his own, and that he needs to be patient as he waits for God to fulfill his promises to his people. And he trusts that God will fulfill those promises. He does not despair—he trusts.

EXPLORE MORE
Read Luke 7 v 1-10. How does the centurion look to Jesus, wait for Jesus, and trust Jesus? He understands that only Jesus can help him—despite his power and influence, he himself cannot heal his servant. He is willing for Jesus to set the agenda. And he trusts that, though he does not deserve Jesus' help, Jesus can and will speak powerfully to change the situation. He knows he himself cannot solve the problem—but he looks to Jesus with hope.

7. Read Mark 15 v 33-39. In what way did the Son of God's experience prove to be the opposite of what Micah had so confidently asserted in Micah 7 v 7? On the cross, we hear Jesus' cry of lament: "My God, My God, why have you forsaken me?" Notice here that Jesus did not cry out for a physical remedy. What he did cry out for was the nearness of God. He cried out for his presence.

But the Father was silent. Micah had confidently asserted that God would hear his prophet; but at the cross, God did not respond to his own Son.

The Father's silence was, of course, not an indication of his inability. He chose not to act. Father and Son both knew that Jesus had to go through this guilt-bearing process for people who were too blind to see their need for it and who, even when they do start to see their desperate situation, do not have the ability to save themselves. For this, the Father and Jesus experienced the reality and agony of the eternal separation that we each deserve. For this, Jesus cried out the most heartrending lament in all of history.

8. What will happen, in the end, to:
• God's people?
- v 8-9: They will rise again, after they fall; they will come out of darkness and into light, and so enjoy vindication (despite their sin).
- v 11: The land of God's people, far from being taken away, will become larger.
- v 14-15: God's people, under their shepherd's rule, will experience the marvel of abundant blessing.
- v 19: God will compassionately remove their sins far from them.
- v 20: They will experience the fulfillment of God's promises to their forefathers— what God swore to Jacob and Abraham, he will do.

• God's enemies?
- v 10: They will experience the shame of defeat.
- v 16: They will realize that however powerful they are, they cannot stand against God or defeat his people.
- v 17: Therefore, they will tremble before God

9. What will God's treatment of his people reveal about God himself (v 18)?
That he is unique. Micah is showing us a God who will keep his promises, who will pardon his people, whose steadfast love will not run dry, and who will remove his people's sins.

10. Read Romans 3 v 21-26. How does God both justly punish his people's sin, and compassionately forgive and restore his people? Through the cross, where, because God went on trial and bore our judgment in our place, God's justice is satisfied, and so the court is adjourned and

we walk free. God came and took our place, and bore our punishment, "so that he might be just and the justifier of the one who has faith in Jesus" (Romans 3 v 26).

Jesus is the one who is full of majesty and is just; but at the same time, he is willing to show us mercy because he has justified us through his work on the cross, by bearing the justice of God himself.

11. The name Micah means "Who is like God?" which is the question he asks in verse 18. What is the answer, and why? No one. No one else is so committed to holiness, to seeing justice done for the poor, oppressed, and vulnerable; and yet is so committed to extending mercy that they are prepared to die for those who live as their enemies in order to bear that justice themselves, and remove the punishment for those who deserve it. We do not find such perfect holiness and such lavish grace in any other "god," nor in any other human—it is only in this God, who came to earth as Jesus, "full of grace and truth" (John 1 v 14). No one is like this God, who can be a just God but also a merciful God.

12. APPLY: If we forget either the reality and seriousness of our sin, or the completeness of our forgiveness, how will this affect:
• our relationship with God?
(1) We will be very complacent and entitled in our attitude to God. We will, deep down, feel that we deserve his blessing and that we have every right to look forward to eternal life. We will not be grateful to him, and when we face difficulties, instead of remembering that without his mercy we deserve far worse, we will grow bitter toward him, thinking that we deserve better than he is giving us. We will never say sorry and repent.

(2) We will live crushed by our failings, and remain distant from God; or we will live in fear, wondering what he thinks of us; or we will go around trying to "make up for" our sins through doing good, but never enjoy the approval and love that God extends in forgiveness.

- **our relationship with others? (Hint: The way we relate to God tends to shape the way we interact with those around us.)**

(1) We will not truly repent when we sin against others. We will make excuses or seek to blame others. And when others sin against us, we will be very quick to grow angry with them and look down on them, because we have forgotten that we are no better. We'll never seek to change out of a desire not to hurt someone again.

(2) We will never really forgive others, or believe that we have been forgiven by another, because that is not the way we relate to God or think God relates to us. So instead of extending forgiveness, we will hold on to a grudge, or only forgive conditionally ("I forgive you, but you had better not do it again"); and instead of receiving forgiveness, we will try to work off our guilt or prove we deserve the love of the person we've wronged.

13. APPLY: If you had to sum up in a sentence what the Holy Spirit has shown you through the prophet Micah as you have studied his book, what would it be? Encourage your group to write their own answers down before sharing them with the rest of the group.

Dig Deeper into Micah

MICAH FOR YOU

In this book from the popular *God's Word For You* series, Stephen brings his trademark insights and real-world applications out of Micah. Written for Christians of every age and stage, whether new believers or pastors and teachers, each title in the series takes a detailed look at a part of the Bible in a readable, relevant way.

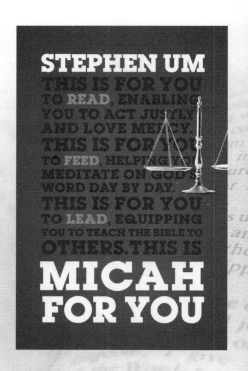

Micah For You is for you:

- *to read*, mapping out the themes, promises and challenges of the book.
- *to feed,* using it as a daily devotional, complete with helpful reflection questions.
- *to lead,* equipping small-group leaders and Bible teachers and preachers to explain, illustrate and apply this wonderful book of the Bible.

Find out more at:
www.thegoodbook.com/for-you

with Stephen Um

EXPLORE DAILY DEVOTIONAL

These Bible readings help you open up the Scriptures, and will encourage and equip you in your walk with God. Available as a book or as an app, *Explore* features Stephen's notes on Micah, alongside contributions from trusted Bible teachers including Timothy Keller, Mark Dever, Tim Chester, Albert Mohler, Jr., Sam Allberry, and Ray Ortlund.

Find out more at:
www.thegoodbook.com/explore

Good Book Guides
The full range

Galatians: 7 Studies
Timothy Keller
ISBN: 9781908762559

Ephesians: 10 Studies
Thabiti Anyabwile
ISBN: 9781907377099

Ephesians: 8 Studies
Richard Coekin
ISBN: 9781910307694

Philippians: 7 Studies
Steven J. Lawson
ISBN: 9781784981181

Colossians: 6 Studies
Mark Meynell
ISBN: 9781906334246

1 Thessalonians:
7 Studies
Mark Wallace
ISBN: 9781904889533

2 Timothy: 7 Studies
Mark Mulryne
ISBN: 9781905564569

Titus: 5 Studies
Tim Chester
ISBN: 9781909919631

Hebrews: 8 Studies
Justin Buzzard
ISBN: 9781906334420

James: 6 Studies
Sam Allberry
ISBN: 9781910307816

1 Peter: 5 Studies
Tim Chester
ISBN: 9781907377853

1 Peter: 6 Studies
Juan R. Sanchez
ISBN: 9781784980177

1 John: 7 Studies
Nathan Buttery
ISBN: 9781904889953

Revelation 2–3: 7 Studies
Jonathan Lamb
ISBN: 9781905564682

TOPICAL

Man of God: 10 Studies
Anthony Bewes & Sam
Allberry
ISBN: 9781904889977

Biblical Womanhood:
10 Studies
Sarah Collins
ISBN: 9781907377532

The Apostles' Creed:
10 Studies
Tim Chester
ISBN: 9781905564415

**Promises Kept Bible
Overview:** 9 Studies
Carl Laferton
ISBN: 9781908317933

Contentment: 6 Studies
Anne Woodcock
ISBN: 9781905564668

**These truths alone: the
Reformation Solas**
6 Studies
Jason Helopoulos
ISBN: 9781784981501

Women of Faith:
8 Studies
Mary Davis
ISBN: 9781904889526

Meeting Jesus: 8 Studies
Jenna Kavonic
ISBN: 9781905564460

Heaven: 6 Studies
Andy Telfer
ISBN: 9781909919457

Making Work Work:
8 Studies
Marcus Nodder
ISBN: 9781908762894

The Holy Spirit: 8 Studies
Pete & Anne Woodcock
ISBN: 9781905564217

Experiencing God:
6 Studies
Tim Chester
ISBN: 9781906334437

Real Prayer: 7 Studies
Anne Woodcock
ISBN: 9781910307595

thegoodbook
COMPANY

BIBLICAL | RELEVANT | ACCESSIBLE

At The Good Book Company, we are dedicated to helping Christians and local churches grow. We believe that God's growth process always starts with hearing clearly what he has said to us through his timeless word—the Bible.

Ever since we opened our doors in 1991, we have been striving to produce Bible-based resources that bring glory to God. We have grown to become an international provider of user-friendly resources to the Christian community, with believers of all backgrounds and denominations using our books, Bible studies, devotionals, evangelistic resources, and DVD-based courses.

We want to equip ordinary Christians to live for Christ day by day, and churches to grow in their knowledge of God, their love for one another, and the effectiveness of their outreach.

Call us for a discussion of your needs or visit one of our local websites for more information on the resources and services we provide.

Your friends at The Good Book Company

thegoodbook.com | thegoodbook.co.uk
thegoodbook.com.au | thegoodbook.co.nz